A GUIDE ON SPIRITUAL GROWTH

How Should the African American Full Figured Woman Respect Her Inner Self as Well as Her Personal Appearance?

By

Paulette G. Cohen known as "inspiration"

ISBN: 1-4033-1372-5

This book is printed on acid free paper.

1st Books - rev. 04/18/02

Acknowledgements and Dedications:

This book was written by my self-Paulette G. Cohen and spoken through the Spirit within.

First and foremost, I would like to give <u>*Special Thanks* </u>*to God, my parent for life and motivator. Thank you for being my #1 inspiration. Having you throughout my journey is so mesmerizing. Every morning I experience new joy, new life and pure excitement. You have lifted me when I was down. You are my joy! Without you I am nothing!*

Next, I would like to dedicate this book to the memory of my loving mother Fannie L. Cohen and to my wonderful father Maurice Campbell, who has been so good to me since I was a child. He is a great role model and I thank God for him.

To my wonderful children, Terrell my oldest and love child. I am so proud of you son. I am so proud of the man you have become. You are headed in the right direction, with God as your leader. You are a great dad, so keep striving to the success you were born to do and be.

To my youngest two, Dana, my special daughter, mommy is so proud of you. Stay focus as I taught you, and with God and the Spirit within. Your mind is strong, and your heart is soft. I will love you forever. Kenneth Jr. My youngest and most lively, you bring joy to me everytime I see your beautiful face. You're smart as a whip and I see every bit of myself in you. Keep growing in the Christian faith as mommy taught you and the Spirit of your grandma Fannie did me.

To all three of you, I say this: you have never experienced a mother's love, until you have experienced God's. I am your biological mother. God blessed me with you and I thank him. All there is to know I will guide you, but guess who's guiding me? Mommy loves you! Both of us!

To my Aunt Rose you have been like a mother, sister, and best friend to my kids and me. I love you so.

To my dear sisters Glenda and Sandra: Sandra please read my book. I love you.

Glenda, thank you for showing me a long time ago the meaning to giving my life to God. I love you.

To my dear and inspirational friends, we consider ourselves The Five Heartbeats. Floretta, Barbara, Rochelle, and Sarah. Since I have been united with you ladies, I never truly knew what friends were about. We were brought together through the power of prayer. We loved each other, and understand why we came together. Thank you for lifting me up again!

I would like to give a special thanks to a dear friend, Leslie Beatty Johnson; this lady I have known since I was 17. We became friends and now I know why. She is a blessing and never turned her back on me, despite the fact we are not always in touch with one another. I love you girl!

Mae Catherine Moore, who has been like a mother and a friend to me, I just want to say thank you for supporting me on this wonderful project. Thank you for understanding why it was so important for me to write this book.

To all my friends at Harlem Hospital Center, Wanda Davis, Marcie Townsend, Sonia Barnes, David Haughton, Nathaniel Rouse, and those out they're who knew of this project or shall I say job that have been in the work for God. I would like to say thank you all so much from the bottom of my heart for really believing in me. It's so amazing to know there are people like you who still believe in people like me.

Finally to the Spirit within, giving the words you chose for me to write sends a glow to my heart. I am so open to all you have said, not only today, always. Thank you God in me!

Contents

Introduction

Upon writing this book, I new there was something in life that was made for me to do. I kept thinking to myself, "wow, what do I want to be when I grow up?" well, guess what? That was about a year ago today, now I'm 37.

Sometimes people still don't know what their career move will be and they could be a little younger or older than I am, but whenever the time comes you will know.

Today I know the efforts and the abilities that I have to achieve the best in life, and it's far from what I thought it would be, but I feel it's the greatest career movement anyone could ask for.

As I began to write this short book, I observed a lot of things about people. People who stood out for all sorts of reason, people in my eyes I felt were in search of the many hidden treasures life has to offer, and most of all, people who want to be more to themselves but don't know how.

Many of these people were women, not just any kind of a woman, women with a great uniqueness and ability to get more than they think they deserve. Women who share a common bond with others like themselves. They are African American Full figure Women.

I studied so much on us and I always wondered why? Why so many issues surrounded the type of people we are, and how discredited we are in society eyes.

Upon my observance, I notice hurt, pain, envy, stress, weariness, and pure look of hopelessness. In my subcontious mind, I said "Why don't they keep themselves up better?" I have experienced women being stared at, laughed at, people insult them, make up rumors, and sometimes they become a common office joke. The pain we feel exceeds more than anything a person could imagine.

Some girls as young as 10 have been through more humiliation than women have in their whole lifetime. It's a very sad thing to be a part of.

One day I knew if I could find a way to bring about joy, not just any kind of common joy, joy that will exhilarate someone so much, they couldn't even imagine they were who they were once.

The Spirit of Gods holiness came to me and said, "we need you to form a program". I did not know where to start, so God, being my mother/father, best friend, confidant, brother/sister, I always turn to. Asked him to give me some ideas. Well, needless to say he not only gave me ideas, he guided me with the Spirit throughout its entirety. He is so amazing!

Well I want to say this, it can happen to you ladies also, and if there is a man out there who feels he falls in this category, please continue to read on. I am here to shed some light upon many hearts out there, whether you are black, white, man, women, or child.

Thanks be to God he brought me about this project, so ladies, here it is. We all have lessons, which need to be told. Do you want to hear mines?

Lesson One.
How to Make Your self-improvement Better in Your Eyes (not Anyone Else's)

I'm going to explore ideas on how to help young and older women on how they can and should perceive themselves although they are full figured. Respect goes along way, and if we as individuals do not look out for each other and ourselves we will never gain the best opportunities in life that is out there to offer us. Lets get started:

Three ways I am advising into looking to venture in search of: Sometimes it is necessary to look to another to better ones self. Remember that it's ok to listen upon another. This is all about learning, loving, and having control of you.

Author H. Jackson Brown Jr. says: Our thoughts determine our responses to life. We are not victims of the world, to the extent that we control our thoughts we control the world.

Maya Angelou, an inspiring black author, poet and screen performer gives a strong opinion of the black women. She states "Black women have not historically stood in the pulpit, but, that doesn't undermine the fact that they built the churches and maintain the pulpits".

For all you ladies and little ladies out there I want you to look into this section closely. Self-improvement is a must for all of us. I am going to dig deep within the soul to reach out to all of you sisters.

Listen to the lessons, learn what you can, take it all in and believe in yourself.

These lessons are just for you!

Part 1

Getting Your Emotions in Shape!

We as black women have a strength we don't even realize the deepness of it. Our inner and outer emotions have outdone all, however if we do not recognize this, we will show it in many ways. There are different ways to perceive you. The right way to do it is center your life in the circle of the love of God! God is our <u>source</u> for all that we do. Once you have established God to be the key to your life force, it will be easy to move on in this lesson.

Now, that may not be easy for everyone to do, it depends on where you want to be. I do not expect everyone to feel the same way as the other but we must establish some type of foundation for ourselves, whether it is to

Communicate with other individuals, who have found themselves, or to educate ourselves with material that may show us different options.

There are so many different thoughts that can come to our minds if we all work as a

4

group and know that we have one another to fall back on in times of need, and most of all we have God as our leader and source throughout all of our troubles or what we call trouble.

Self-awareness being the first thing that we have in mind. Know who we are and what we mean to ourselves. Now the question is: How do we do that? Self worth is a very important factor we must establish from the beginning. What does it mean for us to know how worthy we are as women? Not only as women, as strong African American Full figured women. What do we have to offer one another as this particular person? Take a look inside of yourself and see the inner beauty God has put before you. If you can't see it, then let me show you how:

When we were born into this world we were all blessed with something different from the rest of us and that was individuality. We are all not the same. We can't be because there are no two people who are alike, however, what we all have is Christ. Yes Christ, however, how we receive him is different from the next. He is open to all of us. *We have that gift, and, we must learn how to except him to our best advantage. When we turn things over to Christ being our Savior and God our father of source, it's so amazing the outcome of many magnificent learning's we can accomplish.*

Lets start by opening up our minds, body, and soul. We have just begun the most important process.

The next step is real easy, with all the thought process I just gave you; you will have no problem allowing the following to fall into place.

Beauty comes from within so we are not going to talk about true outer beauty because it does not exist if you can't exert beauty from within first, and that starts with the above process.

Knowing that you are beautiful from the inside will show others how wonderful you are. This is no matter what size you may be. How worthy you are to God is the key to loving yourself and knowing what you are deserving of.

After this process, you are there. You have just crossed the line to establishing beginner's point.

John; 16:8-13

And when he is come, he will reprove the world of sin, and of righteousness, and of judgement.

Of sin, because they believe not me:

Of righteousness, because I go to my Father, and ye see me no more.

Of judgement, because the prince of this world is judged.

I have yet many things to say unto you, but ye cannot bear them now.

* Howbeit when he, the Spirit of truth, is come, he will guide you into all truth; he shall not speak of himself, but whatsoever he shall hear, that shall he speak; and he will show you things to come.

Paulette G. Cohen known as "inspiration"

Part 2

Learning to Love Ourselves from Within

As spoken to you before in Part 1 we discussed the inner self-being one of the first stages to focus the outer self. Well let's talk about the inner-self a little more.

We already have begun the process of loving ourselves, after all that's what this is about. When we learn to love ourselves from within, we learn to love others much better in the near future or if there is someone in our lives already. Loving yourself is so very important in order to love someone else. Listen to me carefully. If you love yourself, you will become a very good lover to someone else. Why? Because, you are secure within and will present yourself to the next one much more openly and positively in order to make a relationship a better one.

I have observe more and more people everyday who just do not like themselves, oh let me re-phrase what I just said, they appear to dislike the entire world. Is this you or maybe someone you know? Everyday is a challenge for them to go through. The world appears to be on their shoulders. Do you know anyone of that nature?

We know sometimes it may be hard to smile on a 24-hour period, but isn't it harder to frown on a 2-hour period? The energy we spend on frowning, being angry, or even acting in a sarcastic way can be used for something more energizing like reading, focusing on the best in life or learning to be a better person.

Lets get into what disturbs someone so much that it overfills that person with anger, at the point where they must be in control of everyone and everything. I know it is different for each person, but lets generalize on the most significant things. Sometimes people who lack self-confident and self-control must be in charge of everything in order to make themselves somebody. This is their way of telling the world in some sort to acknowledge that they exist. Let me give you and example: Sometimes these people feel there is nothing that is important about their life that they must show everyone they can make a difference in their lives by telling them what to do. **Granted** most people (especially in the work force) already know what to do and really do not need anyone to tell them. But, this person still feel the need to let everyone know that they are here and you must and will abide by what they say or else. In reality this is not a threat to anyone but themselves, the fact is they feel they have to have power over you to make you feel discomfort, but actually they are the only one feeling that way. What I am saying is they feel threatened themselves that is why their actions are unspeakable.

How do we deal with this? What I am about to say, may not be believed by everyone, but I will tell you anyway. There is a force in all of us that is guided into our lives by the Holy Spirit. The kingdom of God is in all of us, therefore what we have to do is keep our heads up and say "The God in me bless the God in you"!, and the force from you will enter them and will eventually seize their negative action at some point, for some people who are very hard on themselves, and I say themselves because they really are not hard on anyone else because the impact is right back to them.

You know how it feels to have people dislike you so much that they avoid being in around you for whatever reason? That is what happens when you portray this type of person. You can help these individuals: there is no such things as unsolvable salvation. We all have salvation. God is our salvation! Jesus is our salvation! It is time to start right now! Lets go about receiving him. Let's do it the right way.

We as a group are here to help one another. I am here to help you, whoever you are. Sometimes we do not like to admit that our souls and minds are not at rest, but it's ok. There is always something that is going to try to damage our inner selves but, if your force (the one I mentioned earlier) is there, <u>nothing and I do mean nothing</u> can and will stand in your way.

We have a precious life force. The protection is there but you must acknowledge you want to receive it in order to realize how that protection works for you. It can only work if you allow it to flow through your

body. God will forgive your sins, just asked him to. I know when you tell people this they say we do not want here anything about religion, but, let me tell you this. Spirit is not about religion. It's about willing to receive. Just like you are willing to receive what I am offering to you. Lets try to learn from each other on how to help one another. God is with all of us. He is working through each individual different from the next, so lets go about trying to give a little something extraordinary to the next person that we have.

Job; 42:1-6
Then Job answered the Lord, and said
I know that thou canst do every thing.
and that no thought can be withholden from thee.
Who is he that hideth counsel without knowledge?
Therefore have I uttered that I understood not;
things too wonderful for me, which I know not.
Hear, I beseech thee, and I will speak;
I will demand of thee, and declare thou unto me.
I have heard of thee by the hearing of the ear;
but now mine eye seethe thee;
Wherefore I abhor myself and repent in dust and ashes.

Part 3

What We Are Searching For

We are beginning to grow within these last few pages, learning about what we did not know even exist. Isn't that something to find out? So let's go over what we learned: Spirit is within. Why? Because God is in all of us. We must change our inner selves by loving within first , before we could change our outer selves. Always stay positive! Never think about the worst, only focus on the best. You are beautiful! Life can be beautiful if you allow yourself to flourish. We must be good to ourselves. Know what you are deserving of, and that is everything. Always bless the enemy. Practice the exercises in the up coming lessons. Keep your confidence level up, because you are a child of God and that's something to be proud of.

Now, since we have gone over this, lets move on. Sisters, What do you want out of life? Doesn't matter how old you are, it does not mean you don't want some type of change. Well, where do you want to start?

Look at your life. What do you want to change in your life? It may be personal or even professional, however, once you receive that spiritual growth, all of this will come natural to you. You will know what you want out of life and what you are deserving of. But, let's speak hypothetically! Some of us are in search of the ever lasting: well we already spoke on that. Next, we want continued happiness, we got that. You are happy at who you have become. If you are not married, there is some chance with the positive light that you shine now that you will get that special someone. But, remember, you have become a different person therefore, some things that you sought after before, does not exist in your life anymore. You want the best, remember that. You want to make more money. Well, as I said before, how you exert yourself is how people see you, no matter what type of job you are looking for. Lets search for the best. You want to get into politics? Concentrate on where you want to go and just do it.

The most important thing we must remember to do is, whenever there is a question on what we want, turn it over to God for the answer. Sometimes we are just not sure where to go on something. Most of the time as I stated before, if you are not sure about anything you are about to do, or somewhere you are about to go or even somebody who have suddenly entered your life, please go by your first instincts. You may be right. What I mean is, if there is Mr. New who see you shine and decides to get interested in you, no matter if you have known this person for a long time, or he just all of a sudden appeared in your life, if it does not feel right from the start, be very aware if this is right for you. People will see you differently once your awareness takes place.

The question remains can they handle this about you? Most of the time someone who can relate to your spirituality is basically the type of person you might have to deal with most of the time, however, you will be tempted by some who are not such, but will pretend to be.

It is such a joy to be a child of God! Love it! Enjoy it! Soak it up! This is real life love of you. Now, don't misinterpret what I am saying, as being arrogant or conceited, there is a difference! You will see. Don't you let anyone tell you any different? It is what it is! You are blessed! Girl! You are blessed!

I'm not going to say life is to short so enjoy it. My motto is life is what you make it. Life is good, and if you don't believe it then take a good look at yourself.

I think I have introduced some great things we have to learn about ourselves. Now, the ball is in your court. You have to know how to use it. So let's use it!

Ok, we are going off to another thing girls! What turns you on? Now, now lets not think of the obvious! What in your life makes you excited? Is it working at a new job? More Money? Being in love? What is it that makes you want to achieve and move on to the next thing? Think carefully now because remember what I said, your thought has become a powerful part of what is put before you. You can bring about things you just did

not expect to happen. Therefore be careful of your thoughts.

It's important to observe what you really want for yourself. Let's talk marriage? Committing yourself to someone for the rest of your life takes a tremendous decision. So be careful of who you choose. Ask yourself this: What kind of mate am I looking for? I am not going to tell you how to pick someone who can be in your life, because that is your own personal choice you have to make, however I will advise you on this: Be very careful who you put in your life when your spirituality lifts up. Be sure if you find that right person, he/she will understand where you are coming from, so they will know what is important to you in your personal and spiritual growth. Now, ladies I'm not trying to tell you what to do. You know sometimes in life we just pick people, who are not for us, because we want to be in a relationship so bad, that we choose mates to fulfill our emptiness. Knowing God in your life fills any type of void that may exist!

The next things is about your work experience:

Are you satisfied with what you are doing?

Can you see yourself moving along with what you are doing today, tomorrow also? If not, what do you think should happen?

Well, it depends on what more you want out of life. I can speak very clear on what I want, but it has not been easy. When God told me to do something, which required only my particular skills (my calling), a skill that God has appointed and blessed each person with when they were brought into this world. We all have a calling, however sometimes late in life they come to us, but rest assure, it can happen at anytime. That's Gods work and when he decides he needs you, you must and will answer!

What you can do is ask God what can you do for him? Sometimes it's good to know what you were born to do. You may or may not find out, Just be patient!

Psalms; 31; 1,3-5
In thee O Lord, do I put my trust,
let me never be ashamed;
deliver me in they righteousness.

Paulette G. Cohen known as "inspiration"

for thou art my rock and my fortress;
Therefore for thy name's sake lead me and guide me;
Pull me out of the net me, O Lord God of truth.
that they have laid privily for me;
for thou art my strength.
Into thine hand I commit my spirit;
thou hast redeemed

Lesson 2

Opening our Hearts for Forgiveness

Have there ever been times when you think to yourself "I am such a nice person, why do things happen to me"? I never think things just happen to a person. One of two things can contribute to the main factor or sometimes both. We allow a lot of energy to exert from us for things uncalled upon. That is, we know something is not for our best interest, yet we want to include it in our lives so bad we continue to take it. The other fact may be, God has a plan out for us not to experience something negative but for us to trust in him to make our faith stronger.

Dr. Frederick Eikerenkoetler says: "You had better learn how to forgive yourself and how to forget past mistakes. This isn't yesterday, today"

" When you forgive yourself and turn from your error, then God forgives you"

Paulette G. Cohen known as "inspiration"

"As black and a woman in society systematically orchestrated to oppress each and both, we have a very particular vantage point and therefore have a special contribution to make to the collective intelligence to the literatures of this historical moment".

Toni Cade Babbara; Writer and author of The Black woman, Tales and Stories for Black Folks.

Palms; 32; 1-2
Blessed is he whose transgression is forgiven.
whose sin is covered
Blessed is the man unto whom the
Lord imputeth not iniquity, and in whose
Spirit there is no guile.

Part I

Paulette G. Cohen known as "inspiration"

Leaving Your Troubles in the Lap of Your Higher Power.

What I want you lovely ladies to understand is God is so good! Sometimes we don't realize what can happen when you say I want to receive you in my life lord! The quality in everything we have is so well groomed. Can you imagine going from gloating to glory just from saying a few words and practicing to live that way? It will not make you boring, bad, or non-exciting. Trust me you will be every bit of exciting without the obvious to help you get there, like alcohol, drugs, or something artificial. What you want is real, and God is real!

I am here to share some things with you, so that you will understand where I am coming from. When I need answers to some specific things going on in my life, I turn to God and asked him "What shall I do lord in this manner"? I wait patiently for his answer, which he usually gives to me right away. You asked me how? Sometimes I receive Gods message through lyrics of songs I have not heard in a long time or maybe never before. Sometimes through the minister in the church who tells me things through his sermon. Ladies, let me say this, if you really want to know what God is saying, then you must and I say must listen out for his words. They can come to you in another direction, like left field but you don't know why. Don't sleep on what God can do. He is our miracle and Jesus was a saint. I have had many troubles in my life, but coming from a Christian background, even I was surprised at some of the encounters I allowed to let happen. We all make mistakes that we regret but let's get a grip on the reality stage. Whatever happens to us is because we allow it to happen! OK? We have to stop blaming others for our wrong doings. There is no person in this world that is perfect except God.

The only thing that we must remember is to <u>Let Go and Let God!</u> He is our maker and there for us. Ask God to help you get yourself together that you may wake up to a better person.

Paulette G. Cohen known as "inspiration"

When we look into the entertainment field so many singers sing about something we really don't like, but most of them always thank God. Can you do that? Actually thank the wonderful man above for all the goodness he has brought to you. You say what? You can't remember what to thank him for? Well, if you can't remember what you should thank him for, guess what? I'm here to remind you!

No matter what size you are, or how much you have, lets start the countdown and when we finish, put a big broad smile on your face.

1. **We were blessed with the presence of being born.**
2. **We all have working limbs, and even if we don't, we have life!**
3. **We have someone on-call 24 hours who is willing to listen to our Troubles without saying shut up!**
4. **We are gathering as a group to help one another. That is sister love.**

28

5. *For those of us who have family, it is a blessing to wake up with them or be in touch with them.*

6. *For those of us who are employed, we have a job to go to.*

7. *We are spiritual beings and that comes from within and this is something also to be grateful for.*

8. *We have somewhere to live, whether it's a shelter or home.*

9. *We have survived through some of the most incredible things that makes us strong.*

10. *If you are reading this book, then you have insight on yourself and want to learn more.*

Now, I know they all may not apply to everyone, but at least five have to be related to most of us out there. So, please don't tell me that you can't see what God has put before you. Wake Up! I am here to show and tell you how to make a difference. At this point things should be clearer in your life and what you have to offer this world.

Being loved is a beautiful thing. The impact it has on a person can be wonderful. Being in love is even better, but knowing that God has such a powerful love is an inspiration that we can't even imagine unless we know how to appreciate it.

Here is a brief exercise I would like to introduce to those of you who never tried it. Get a piece of paper and pencil or pen. What is important in your mind or heart that you really want? If it is more than one thing, that's even better. Now, make a list or if it's only one thing that you really desire you want, then ask God if he will provide this for you. Take that paper and put it where you feel is the safest place for it, (I usually keep mines in the bible preferably the 23 palms) but where ever you feel comfortable.

Now wait! You must be patient when asking God for anything. God knows what we need, it does not mean he will not provide what you want but, if it is not for your best interest then he will not let it happen or give it to you. God protects you. All I say is don't give up on God, because he knows what you need and do not. He also works on his time.

We tend to get very impatient when it comes to getting and answer on what we feel we need in life, but do we really know what we need? We make the mistake of thinking we know everything about what we want but that is not true. Our desires as beings tend to run very thin and sometimes to thick, so let get a grip!

Philippians; 3; 14
I press toward the mark for the prize of the high calling of God in Christ Jesus.

Paulette G. Cohen known as "inspiration"

Part 2

Rebuilding of Your Soul

Some of us have started in a roaring way. We have become so intuned with ourselves that we never thought of the positive affect it would have on our lives. You know ladies; positivity is the enlightenment of our minds. When the thought can be magnified in a specific way that we control our overall being, just imagine what takes place.

It's good to get material that you can now relate to, where you can proceed with another part of this New World that has taken place. I think it's such a lovely thing to be a part of with you ladies. Knowing who we are, sharing familiar worlds, sister to sister acts. Don't you think you have changed? Yes you have!

If some of you are in relationships, that's good! You can pass what you have gained on to whomever you love or have a strong liking too if they are still in search of. You know why? We are all one! The spirit we share is universal. There is a oneness in everybody.

Heaven awaits our answers to what God has to offer us.

The thing I want you also to know is, when enlightened by the spirit, you don't have to ever feel guilty about anything. You will respect yourself so much that you are already conscious of what you are doing and it will be to the best of your interest.

Many of us just don't want to believe we can be saved. There is always going to be doubt somewhere. Know that it can be replace by a magnificent learning that is instilled in all of us. Reach out and touch someone, yourself! It would be to your best interest to feel what you need. You know, it's ok to need someone. I need God and you need God all the time.

To the next thing in order, we must adjust to our self-growth. Growing as strong African American heritage people. The gift of spirituality is awesome! What a gift it can be too! Do you realize what strength black people have as a whole. The way we display ourselves can sometime become a negative impact towards others. Why you say? Because we can get very beside ourselves and look at our brothers and sisters like we are better than they are.

Directing this to the sisters only, have you ever had another sister look you up and down like you got mud on your foot? Meanwhile, the white women are reading the paper or drinking coffee. You see the stigma? Why must we always search to judge someone that we don't even know? Who are we? You never hardly witness a white woman checking out another woman in that sort of manner, and you may never will. Let me re-phrase once again, if a white women looks at another woman you may not know it because they do it in such a fashion that it is not obvious to the other individual.

The competition is very thoughtless out there. Instead of us working or striving to the best of our abilities and sharing what we have learned with others, we knock each other over to get there first. There is NO unity! We are not aware of the other person's feeling at all. Even if we are, we think of the worst way to go about getting something first than the best. We must stop this! Right Now!

Not tomorrow, or yesterday, Right Now! As I said we have to learn to help each other. That's another form of prosperity. What we give of ourselves we will get back double. You will never know where this is coming from if you don't experience true giving. True giving is giving from the heart. Wanting to do what comes naturally to your mind, body, or soul. Wanting to extend your hand where it is needed most. Giving to the needed without a question of where is this going? Cradling a baby whom has no mother to cry to. It's like people who have children. Knowing how hard it can be to raise a child, sometimes we look to our other family members to help. Tell me something, what's wrong with people on the outside of the community or area? We are all in touch with helping young people with their best interest in life? There is nothing wrong! That's unity.

Love in the order that we want to receive it is wonderful, and we must understand if it does not come in the fashion we want, does not mean it won't come. I myself have experience thinking a certain person would be the one I fall in love with and eventually marry. It never winds up that way. Someone you least expect will walk into your life without you looking back on what you may have asked in your heart or out loud to God or maybe just discussing with a friend and you will say "Wow, how did this happen?" It may be someone you already know, or least thought you would get involved with. Whomever this person is most likely will be someone to play a role in a fashion you have wanted for the rest of your life. Be patient!

Lively hood is overwhelmed by the insecurity we have inside. That is why I'm, reaching out to you ladies. Don't make yourself look silly out there. It is and embarrassment to you. Getting in front of people and saying things not in your best interest. Allowing the opposite sex to be better than you.

I am about to give you another scenario. Have you seen people defend the person they are involved with no matter what have been done to them? I'm talking about infidelity. There is no excuse for us to except why someone chooses to sleep with more than one person. This goes out to both sexes. When we begin to justify why we allow that person to do the things we know we don't deserve to have happen to us, something is very wrong. I don't care if that person has one foot in the grave and one on a kickstand: there is no excuse for that type of behavior to be excepted. We are only telling that person as well as everyone else, I'm a door mat, walk over me. You don't even have to wipe your foot.

My theory on inner building process takes place when you open yourself up to say, I need help. There is a growing rush to you. Stop allowing negative energy to fill your mind, where you think this is all I can have. There is no one better for me. I will just settle. I can't do any better than this. We all can do better. I understand some people do not want to be alone in life. You are never alone: you have God with you all the time. He is your friend, he is your mother/father, and he is your ears, eyes, and mouth. Remember he is in you! Knowing that God is in you will enable you to make better choices for yourself.

Ephesians; 4; 4-7
There is one body, and one Spirit, even as ye are called
in one hope of your calling,
one Lord, one faith, one baptism,
one God, and Father of all, who is
above all, and through all, and in y all.
But unto every one of us is given grace according

to the measure of the gift of Christ.

Part 3

Introduction to Meditation w/A Vision of Yourself

Lets get started on ways to get ourselves in better shape with our own emotions. As a group we must think of how to improve our self-abilities. We already have begun the book, let's start the process.

We must begin with deep breathing exercises to one another. This way we will get familiar with our fellow sisters and or brothers who are in need of our love.

I want you to experience the unknown in your entire life. This is genuine love and an order of divine guidance that we must learn from each other. After all, it's proven that we are in search of something, maybe the hidden soul.

Our souls need to be lifted in order for us to find divine guidance! It is our duty as sisters and brothers in search of the divine. I'm here to give you some lessons, so are you ready? You are reading this book because you want to be somewhere right? So, let's get there.

Our minds are wondering right now, and our hearts are open for forgiveness. Close your eyes and ask yourself this:

1. *Do I forgive myself for all the things I have done that may not have been in the best interest of myself?*
2. *Did I do this because I was ready?*
3. *Was I afraid of what my life was about?*
4. *What am I in search of? And, do I even know why I'm in search Of it?*
5. *When I move in the Motion of Order, will I be willing to receive it?*
6. *Will my heart be open to Divine Guidance?*
7. *Am I ready to become a foster sister to others spirituality?*
8. *Am I ready to leave all my troubles in the lap of the Divine Guider?*
9. *Am I ready to except that love conquers all?*

Those are just some questions you may want to ask yourself in order to feel your way through, and make you more aware of what to expect throughout to better your journey.

Now, we must exercise our limbs of life to put our minds in a perspective order. Let us think about something that has been on our mind for a long time that we can't shake what it means to us. Think carefully! Now, what does this particular item, person? Or situation means to you? How important is it to you? Why do you think it is on your mind so heavy?

Meditate on the true actuality of the situation and ask yourself if this is important to me, and should I keep in touch with part of my well being because of the substance of it. Yes that is what it is! You are making the statement to the question so: the next step would be make that particular thought come to process of reality or take it out of your mind.

Sometimes we can continuously concentrate on the inevitable and let it take over our well being, but no matter what it is all about; nothing can be solved until you turn it over to God!

When we put our minds in order, the Divine Order, the strength we receive from the infinite is so electrifying. Therefore, as we come together to one another, sister to sister, brother to brother, and cry our souls out to each other, the voice of the undeniable is received by the infinite so loud and clear that it doubles the outcome of reality to the highest power.

That is why it is so important for all of us to continue to unite as one! We need supportive strength from the above and to recognize how we can help each and everyone out there just like us.

We are not going to talk about the weight process right now. This is not an important factor at this moment. What is important is the building of your soul. Building of your self-esteem, building of the spirit around you. We must learn all these things first before we can begin to do anything superficial. There is no room for egos, only people who are trying to understand. Now to all you beautiful ladies, let's see what's up for us. So you are not a size 10, well guess what? neither am I. Stand up and look at yourself in the mirror right now. What do you see? You see a creature "God said one day I am going to create someone there will never be anyone else like". Here you come! Born to look the best and set out for something wonderful in life to go for.

In all of our lives there is going to be something that we feel we want to have but don't know if we should have it. Personally when this happens to me I go straight to my source and ask his opinion because I know what he feels I am cut out to have and what is right for me, therefore I trust his better judgement on anything out of life that I may feel is good for me. If he comes back to me in so many words and say it is just not right for me I would have to go back to what he has done for me and evaluate the situation carefully and decide if I am going to go about what I want either way. Trust me when I say he knows what is best for you, because, sometimes we may think something is best for us and it is not. I will give you a perfect *example of what I am talking about: I'm sure most of us would like to have that very special someone in our lives that we could spend the rest of our life with and it seems it will never happen. When we start doing something or settling for someone just to be seeing somebody, it never works out. Put your trust in God and realize only he knows what is best for all of us.*

The time is right when he says it is right. Do not try to get into something that is not ethical for you or anyone to whom it may concern.

Deuteronomy; 29; 29
The secret things belong unto the Lord of God: but those
Things which are revealed belong unto us and to our
children for ever, that we may do all the words of this law

Paulette G. Cohen known as "inspiration"

Lesson 3
Meditation-The Process

We have grown closer in spirit as sisters have. The move has already begun for us to go along. We're out there: we have been stripped to the bone. All of our flesh is in tuned for the beginning of some of the most magnifying learning's to be taught.

"Women have a certain sense of primary things like blood, which is life. I think it's because women are connected to such primal things that we have not necessarily a greater facility but a broader vehicle for exploring our experience".
Alexis Deveaux: A freelance
writer, contributing poems and a community worker.

Paulette G. Cohen known as "inspiration"

Part 1.

Getting More Acquainted with Yourself

Let's go about this first: Programming our bodies to fit our minds.

Exercise #1
Meditation: There are different ways to meditate. I suggest dim lights or candles, quiet and alone. Close your eyes and imagine yourself. Look at yourself good. Look at what God felt compelled to bring about in his world. Can you see it? Now, take a deep breath and exhale. Ask yourself inside out what do you need the most? Now wait. Your answer will come. Be patient! Once you get your answer, move on to the next question. You have the right to know what you want to know about you! What makes you so unhappy? While your vision is there, notice the individual techniques about yourself. No one can tell you what that is but you, and the God in you!

What you want to do is get closer to God and your Spiritual awareness. Anyway that is comfortable to you is all needed. Meditation is relaxing to the soul and makes the cells in your body more alert and you more in tuned to what is ailing you.

Deep meditation will make your self-awareness begin.

Clear everything going on in your mind except you and circle of light which will appear.

We must remember all you need to do is be open wanting to be better with ourselves. Our souls will be lifted from all troubles we bare. God loves us. There is no pressure in wanting advice and seeking someone professional to give it to you. We could spend a lot of money on someone that can't give us what we can get for free, and the advice is true, real, and everlasting. God is our therapist. His healing process is on going and you don't have to worry about the time, and how much it is going to cost you.

Doesn't it feel good to have our inner and outer souls massage by the best masseuse in the world? You cannot get this anywhere, but in the presence of reality.

Palms; 63; 5
My soul shall be satisfied as with marrow and Fatness.

Exercise II
Energy: We are positive beings, so let's focus on our energy. Our minds have shown us if we go into deep thought about who we are, it will strengthen our souls, therefore what do you think is going to happen to you if you look into something in a negative way? Or should I say think of something bad. Guess what? If you wish on something bad it will happen. That's why it is so important not to think of you in a negative manner. Always say I am a blessing from God! I am going to bless the enemy. You, knowing who you are and how good it feels to be you, but you have to practice this on a regular schedule. It takes a lot of work to get rid of those negative vibes, around, because, we are always going to encounter the negative being, but you, a spiritual being have the power to push all of it away. Always bless the enemy. Know that you can come to God for anything and be assured he will provide.

Sometimes we get in the habit of wanting things we don't need. We look for the worst to happen and not the best. Do you know what can happen when you strengthen your mind to focus only on the best outlook and not the worst? The best will happen, it only can.

Exercise III
Posture: Stand up straight! Put you arms up in the air and lower them slowly down. Always keep your back straight, chest out, and head up. Lift your arms up and down several times, this helps you to prepare your body to go along with your mind. You can keep doing this for a long as you feel the need to strengthen your body along with your mind. It will also help you to prepare to go about the world with dignity.

Exercise IV
Vision: Look in the mirror nude and say "I am here to stay". I have a lot to offer. I'm blessed, reassured and ready to go about what God has for me to do. When you say this, you are building your confidence as you

talk. The world is here, nothing can get me down, Because I am love and the God in me knows only love.

After we have gone about these four exercises, you have begun the process of cleansing your soul. We must clean ourselves from within to begin a new stage in life. What I am saying is how can we build ourselves from within if we do not get rid of the unnecessary stuff? (That's whatever is pending to make you feel down).

Know that you are opening yourself up to wanting to better you, only makes greater happenings. Now, we may run into some bumpy roads on the way. Why you say? because as I stated before we are around negative energy, which sometimes have a problem with the positive growth, we are trying to achieve, but we are better than that. We have learned how to detect the good from the bad. You have better judgment THAT OPENED YOU UP TO DETERMINE WHAT IS AND WHAT IS NOT. Your eyes have seen this before. Your ears have heard this. You have a keen sense of smell, so. With

all of this awareness you know how to react when something inappropriate occurs.

Are you beginning to love yourself the way you should be loved? That's right, let's go there! Realize this, when you begin to really know what you want, what you are worthy of, what you need once yourself awareness has taken a big turn, your mind is on only providing good. No one can make you feel anything less. You can make love to yourself than be physically battered by a person who does not appreciate him or herself! That's right themselves. They don't like who he or she maybe, therefore they thrust whatever possible on someone innocent or vulnerable, but, you are not this person. You have knowingly strengthened your mind to new heights. You are strong, deserving that you can be a witness. You can go just about any tasks.

Ladies we have so much to give of ourselves, poor quality does not fit in when it comes to men, clothes, positions, or anything less than the best. We perceive ourselves like a magic wand. We are lovely as ever. The beauty is so magnifying. Oh how real! Do you feel it? Can you see it? If you can't, nobody else can. If you see it everyone else will too.

Keep smiling, laughing, being aware, and being positive. Be good to yourself as well as others. The warmness is over whelming and that's so magnifying. This is all about positive energy and the enlightenment of the soul. We are rich in love, spirit, and confidence. Any type of force cannot replace this.

Part II

Allowing the Flow of Love Through your Mind

In time we are going to be related to everyone around us as a whole. The universe is so miraculous that we can do only but feed into the positive light and become one. I want to say to you lovely ladies and gentlemen, if there are any of you who decided to read this book, I am glad you started on the road of peace. To finally come to the conclusion that your life is nothing without God in it, takes a lot of courage. Courage to be able too finally says, "yes I need him so much in my life". It's ok to say that, because it's the beginning of a new happiness.

Once you can let it out verbally that you are nothing without the man almighty himself, my lord, what a great new beginning. He lifts my spirits to the highest mountain. I cannot even imagine my life without him in it. I cannot see myself waking up in the morning without recognizing he's the reason I even woke up.

Love is grand, and even grander when you have God in it. Reach to the stars and the highest power. Know that his ears are open to listen to your troubles. Fear not, because God is the most wonderful person in life there will ever be. Not your mother or your father remembers he is your mother/father. Not your sister or brother, know he is your sister/brother. Not your soul mate, remember he is your soul mate. Not your teacher or preacher, he is your teacher/preacher. Not your best friend, he is your best friend. God is everything to us. That's what makes him so powerful, Because he is all that!

Let me say this to you also, I use to think about everything another person may have felt is not important enough to worry about. I did because I'm the type of person who likes to do things right. I believe in doing whatever is put before me. I don't believe in hurting another individual. I try to be the best in everything I am a part of. My point behind this is, sometimes things are totally out of our hands and we have no control over it, therefore we can get a little upset just the way I did and wonder why things are going that way or won't go the way we would like. Then one day I released all of myself and said "I'm going to let go'! For me to say I would let go meant to physically let go of everything I felt at once was important. All the people in my life who use to agitate me, all the problems I use to worry about, all my financial issues I left on the table, all my personal relationships I let go, all my family problems I prayed upon. Everything went into a big cookie jar the size of a mountain. I shipped it via air prayer to God. Moments after, I received a response in blessings. To say all that is to say this, Let Go! God will see you through life's challenges. You don't have to compete in this game, because it's anyone's game!

In that moment of your life where you find people who want to be ahead of you first for whatever reason, and they begin to step across certain boundaries, you can just let it blow off your shoulders and continue to move along in your own fashion. I don't believe everyone can be the same, however, if you give those ugly issues over to God and let him handle them the correct way, (because his way is the only way), you will live blissfully.

I am probably at the happiest moment of my life now. Not because of any kind of materialistic reasons, but, because I see the wonderful things God has done for me and I know he takes care of any and all of my problems. I know when I come to him he is listening to me. The most comfortable feeling I have is knowing he is around me with his arms open to embrace me. I know the choices I make are because the spirit has allowed them to be there for me. I know people that all of a sudden appear in my life were from God, and the Holy Spirit. I know when something inside says don't do it that's the spirit protecting me. With all this, why would I want to be anywhere else.

I have succumbed my life where God is the head of all. That is my master and I do what I do for him. When I make mistakes, I pick myself up dust myself off, and start all over again. No one in this world but God can make me fear for anything, because I know I am capable of having it all. All that I want out of life is good.

This feeling can overcome to you if you allow it to get in your mind, body, and soul. Take a good look at yourself and ask God to help you, Throughout any of what you feel you need him for. He does not discriminate, he does not judge, he does not pick and choose, he shows no favoritism, he is not picky, he does not care what gender you are. This is all the more reason why you can go to him. Don't you feel better about being around someone like that, rather than all the opposites?

I guess I can say truly the reason I keep repeating myself is because I feel we, as women need to focus more on helping each other out more. That's why I was sent out here to you. To let you know my soul has connected to yours and I was sent to you for reasons God knows best. Why don't you take the time to listen to some of what I am telling you? Trust me that this is true to the word and it does not come just from my mouth, but from the mouth of the Holy Spirit!

"I do believe in blacks writing about black life. There are many aspects of black life, we need to go into further; for instance, the whole church area needs more attention. I'm not just talking about sisters in their wide hats shouting. There's a whole lot going on in the church, and somebody ought to tackle it".
Gwendolyn Brooks,

Writer, Author; Annie Allen, The Bean Eaters and many other Inspiring Novels.

Paulette G. Cohen known as "inspiration"

Part III

Moving Forward

Now, all grown up rich in glory and more particular about who I am and very secure of the being that I will always be. My life has been chosen a long time ago for me. I had no decisions to make except a choice whether to receive the glory of God or go where I thought was right which when made by anyone it usually is not the right thing to do. So, I except the plate of eternal light from the son Jesus and the Divine to be my constant companion in all the choices that I have to make.

As I move forward into my daily routine I reach for even higher goals than anyone may expect. I am telling you ladies this to let you know it's ok to go about your life in this manner. Everyone has a different destination but eternal glory will always be a positive option that you can have if you follow the correct paths in life. I know the love that I have been enriched with has shined and made an even deeper impact on my soul. It can in yours too.

I encourage many people to take risks with their lives by following their heart. Not with just anything but with the decision to move forward with openness to love thyself unconditionally. The results to this will be one of those success stories in your life, if that is what you are searching for. Most of us are. Don't be afraid to let your guards down just a tiny bit. It's ok to enjoy the person you were made to be. I know I am.

I am finally coming to the true realization of what my life is about. I have received the assurance from the man above that the coarse of the path that he chose for me is my destination to a life of joyful happiness. I am in control of my smile, my laughter, and my over whelming joy. It's me! It's me! It's me! Oh Lord! Standing in the sea of love!

Now is the time to know and really know what can and will be in the way if you allow the uncertain. I have grown to look out for the uncertain. I have made my move over to what is so good in life. The God of all being my heavenly divine Guider to unlimited resources in life. This is good! This is real good! Thank you for all this good. Wow, how would you feel if this were you?

The truth is so magnificent because at one time I just knew things were not meant to be. I could not see the forest for the trees and then I finally had to take this sudden turn over to another unlimited source that all my life I knew was there but, I just couldn'' find where it was coming from. When that did happen I just said "thank You'' I am becoming more intuned with the reality of the fulfillment in Gods eye for me, at least in this lifetime.

" I have to fight with myself. I hit my head against the wall because I don't want to know all the terrible things that I know about. I don't want to feel all these wretched things, but they're in me already. If I don't get rid of them. I'm not ever going to feel anything else. When our culture, as a whole, realizes that the act of not saying something does not mean that you're not living it, when this happens, we're going to have dramatic pieces, all kinds of art that are so rich. Nitozake Shange;

Lesson 4
How to Carry Yourself

Sometimes in life we can look as good as ever but don't know exactly what it means to look good. Beauty is in the eyes of the beholder. Think about you and who holds this wonderful world we live in. It is important for us as African Princesses to possess beauty in the way we have learn through spirit. Not only by what you wear but what you say. Let's dig deep into our wardrobe of uncertainty and find out just the right way to do this:

"We who are black have to recognize our basic powerlessness, and that's strength". Nikki Giovanni:

Paulette G. Cohen known as "inspiration"

Part 1.

Paulette G. Cohen known as "inspiration"

A Self Portrait to be displayed

With clothing we must know our limitations, which is presented to us out there. When it comes to large women's clothes they don't give us a great choice. What is best for you? Let's see: Me being a large busted and hip/thigh area woman, what should I wear? My self image and how important is that to me. Well, lets talk. We know that they have clothes out there to fit me. NO PROBLEM! But, what type of clothes? Am I the conservative one? Or am I liberal in my dress style? Liberal or conservative we must watch how we wear our clothes. Being large in many areas than the average size can be very deceiving for a woman wanting to look her best, whether conservative, liberal, or sexy to sleazy. Let's talk! What's right for you. We already established the beauty we show from within, now the beauty from the outside. God has blessed us with more to love, and what's wrong with that? I say nothing! The question is, Are you happy with that look? If yes, let's just move on. If no, then its time to work on a little in between matters. What's that you say? Losing those excess pounds you are not happy with. Does this sound like you? if so where do you start? Well let's see how much and where do you want to drop those pounds? Whatever you do just set your mind in focus and lets go. Eating right usually is the best way but who am I to say I'm not trying to lose weight. I have grown to be happy for who I am and live my life to the fullest to gain and achieve success the best way possible with my inner self. However, for those who would like to lose, I encourage you to not take dramatic measures to get rid of pounds quickly. Go to a doctor, but, always say a little prayer and ask God almighty to help you the best way.

Now, back to those who are willing to work with who they are today. Motivation is a good way to start the process of trying to establish anything good out of life. That starts with prayer. Prayer is the key to becoming motivated. Once that action has taken place then you know where you want to go.

Girls, ladies, women, let me tell you something, When God blessed us he did it and did it well. There are so many wonderful things and places for people out there like us, it's just a matter of going for it. Know yourself, strut yourself, and hold yourself up to the highest level as possible. Let everyone know we are here and we will not settle for anything less.

Clothing oh let me tell you there are many clothes out there, but where do we go? Catalogs are a start for finding the most successful stores specializing in the full figured woman. Style polyester is usually what is put before the larger size woman, and I will tell you why: It is figured that since we are of this size we have to squeeze into something that we can get into. So what is put out there is a stretch type material made to make us feel confortable. The question is are we really comfortable wearing that type of stuff? The quality is what I tend to have a problem with. If the style is in for polyester then "hey who can say?" However, if that is all there is to offer because society feels, well, as long as it fits then buy it. Not! We can fit a lot of other material, it depends on you. Know what you deserve and search for the best. It does not have to cost you your arm, leg, head, and most of all, a lot of money to look good, it depends on you.

Now we know certain styles out there are just not for us! You know that. For example: Some spandex is just not appropriate for us gals. Some jeans are not for us. Why you asked? Let me tell you, because if you have a broad and expanded backside, hipline, or larger than the normal waistline, it's just not the right look for you. Don't misinterpret what I'm saying, denims can make a thin woman's butt look larger than it is. So what do you think it would do to a woman of size?

This is where the pride takes place in our image. We want to be respected in the utmost way as possible, therefore let's represent! Show the world we know how to look good and feel good with what we have been blessed with. If you as a person do not understand, let me just elaborate a little more. We don't need to show the world we are overly blessed in certain areas; therefore there is no need to have something showing you're whatever hanging out. There are plenty of other materials, which are much more flattering and show the figure a little more in the eccentric way. Now, how eccentric do you want to look? You asked? Full figured women have a special and unique way about themselves. How we carry it is the story. Listen to me carefully. No matter how tall or large you are, does not mean you can't stand out as one of the most beautiful women out there. Remember what I said earlier, the inner self is so very important to recognize. We don't care who on the outside don't recognize it, as long as you know it, You asked why? Simply because if you know this yourself, then you will do nothing but shine on the outside. Self-esteem is a must in getting you into different areas of your life, whether it's to get a job, a man, into politics or whatever. Knowing you are a gift from God and what you have to offer not only as a woman but a strong black woman is very and I say very important to becoming successful or to gain the respect you are deserving of.

Gets use to this: Learn to love yourself. This will help you to keep yourself on the right track to success and happiness the way you want it. Practice getting up and going straight to a mirror and saying aloud, I have learned to love myself for who I am. The God in me has blessed others, as I am the same way. We are helping each other out at this point. You asked why? Because we have just helped another by blessing the God in us as a whole. Then raise your arms up in the air and say 'A new day has come for me to show the world how beautiful I am once again".

After you have finished your regular morning duties before you go about your journey, you will step into the world with a broad smile knowing wherever you are headed is the beginning of a beautiful day. Bare in mind that life is what you make it. If you walk out with a frown your day will be none than less than a miserable day. If you walk out feeling confident and happy, guess what? You will have the most magnificent day that God has to give to you. Learn to depend on God who makes all things possible.

Paulette G. Cohen known as "inspiration"

You may say this:

Palms 25:1-3
Unto thee, O Lord, do I lift up my soul.
O my God, I trust in thee,
let me not be ashamed.
let not mine enemies triumph over me.
Yes, let none that wait on thee be ashamed:
let them be ashamed which
transgress without cause.

Part II

Working on the Being that you are

Life can be a beautiful thing; we just have to allow it to filter throughout our bodies.

Here are some important points we must begin to follow to allow ourselves to become in tunes with the inner part of our being:

1. *Pray before you go about any task.*
2. *Talk to a friend whom you can trust with only a positive out look.*
3. *Give careful thought to what you are to yourself.*
4. *Know how important you are to yourself*
5. *Meditate on what is important to you.*
6. *Be willing to accept a strong wind of words that will come your Way (and it will come).*
7. *Be very careful of your thoughts that you may be able to determine the negative from the positive*
8. *Eliminate unnecessary images in your mind.*

9. *Don't look at anything that is not good for you before you go to bed.*
10. *Don't be wary about everything; trust your first instinct.*

It might be a little difficult to allow some of these things to take place in your life, however, everything I am talking about is for you to build from. We are about building our self worth, self-esteem.

You may say to yourself, what does this have to do with being a full figured woman. Well, let me tell you, a lot! Some people have put it through our minds that we are less of a person because we are in their eyes too fat, too large, too big, to wide, or whatever they can say that will insult you. Whenever this happens you will know how to handle it, without being very down on yourself. Sometimes if we don't acknowledge our self worth we wind up letting other people talk down on us in a viscous way and make us feel we are less than they are. We can use our mind over matter. So, lets try to do that. Mind over matter, what is that you say? It means your mind is in total control over your well being: therefore it does not matter what other people are saying. You are a gift from God! How important you are to yourself depends on what you feel about you. I know myself worth. I know I can make a difference in lot of people's lives.

We all have special qualities we exert. Remember in Lesson 1, I spoke about all of us being born with something different from the next, and that was individuality. Well, the same applies to having something special within you. Sometimes it takes all of us a little time to realize what that is exactly. On the other hand, it can come to us in many different ways, like an all of a sudden job, which becomes yours, FOR LIFE! This means that you will continue to do this throughout the period you are alive. Don't ever think when you are given a specific job that it is negative, because it is NOT. Only good can come out of a special calling. You are helping someone or something good. Always remember that you can also develop a good learning experience from this job that

will enable you to move on better in your own personnel spiritual growth.

Everything I am trying to teach you is all about you! You know who you are, and I know who some of you are too. That's why I am writing this. So, open yourselves up to only what can and will be good for you.

Sisters, let's go about this the right way and what is the right way you say? Everything in both parts of my chapters from beginning to end. You will see such a change in your life that you won't ever look back, and attraction let me tell you about attraction. The energy you exert from yourself will be so magnifying that you won't only attract metal, but the opposite sex will do only one thing and that is RESPECT and worship the person you will have become.

Now, you have the look of a lovely person. Someone that people have only dreamed of, however, they did not know how to go about talking too. The type of person that only the worthy can appreciate. Do not expect a knucklehead or should I say someone who has not found themselves to be able to adapt to the type of person you have become. The way you will exert yourself will be so exciting and new to people who have known you forever, because of the change that have naturally taken place.

Let's start right now women! Don't Wait! Life is good, but guess what? The best is yet to come!

Luke: 17:5-6
And the apostles said unto thee Lord,
Increase our faith
And the Lord said, If ye had faith as a grain Of mustard seed, ye might say unto this sycamine tree, Be thou plucked up by the root, and be thou planted in the sea;
and it should obey you.

Paulette G. Cohen known as "inspiration"

Part III

Looking Through the Mirror of Your Soul

As you can see, this guide can be aimed at anyone. Although my main focus is on beautiful and wonderful African American Woman of size, we know that no matter what culture, size, or sex you are, this maintains to you as well. The point behind it is, love thyself before you love anyone else. It is hard enough trying to adopt to the issues that surround all that's behind being who you are. Learning the significant reasons to love you first is a must.

Let me break it down to you sisters like this, when we exert ourselves in a way that is totally out of line to begin with, and dress all above and way out to suit the other individual, guess what that tells people? It says I really don't care what you think, I look good! That may be the way to think as part of being positive about who you are, but! What kind of message are you truly sending out to the public, your family, friends, and

90

whoever? This is when you ask yourself, do I love me? Or what is the meaning of loving myself? When you have established the fact you love yourself, you will dress to impress in a different manner. The way you walk and the way you talk will be a show of dignity.

I have notice in particular, men who really know how to feel good about themselves. The saddest thing about this is, men choose to be very careful about who they put in their lives as a girlfriend or even more so as their wife. They observe things we don't even know they are checking out. Some men of course choose women based on their nationality mainly, or, it could be because of their body or whatever is physical.

Now mind you I'm not saying that is the way to pick someone to be in your life. As a matter of fact, I think those reasons are the worse. I hope you know God has made the choice for us long before we ever knew about it. No matter who you may feel is your quote on quote soul mate, may not be. Look back into your life and if you have dated before, been married, or had a good friend/compa- nion that all of a sudden the relationship split for whatever reason can be a disappointment. Starting all over again is hard work, but what is good about it is you can look back on what may have been done wrong and you can correct yourself to proceed with the next relationship in a more positive manner trying not to repeat what you failed to do in the others.

Everytime you end a relationship of some sort does not mean you did something so wrong. It just was not for you. That day will come, and never settle for less. You know what you desire and deserve, therefore keep searching until you get what you want. This does not mean literally look for someone just be more alert and aware of people you do not want to get involved with. A lot of times we make excuses to be with someone to justify why we except what is handed over although we know this is not for us.

Pray for all your moves, especially in relationships. God will never disappoint you. I'm sure he has someone very good in store for you in the future, just believe in him and especially believe in yourself.

I spoke to you in one of my last chapters about God being your source. Sometimes I go through periods of why certain things happen to me in reference to my finances, and I say well, let's not go there! I don't get my finances from my work place; I get it from God. To develop that frame of mind takes a good amount of your inner self-being on display. What I mean by this is it's all right to poor out your thoughts to someone else, it's a good exercise and will help your spiritual building process. Think about when you go to your job, school, church, or wherever. Why besides the obvious are you going? When you get there, why are you proceeding to the things you have too? There is one answer and one answer only; you know what that is? Because God has allowed you to make that move to those places and said you must proceed with your life in this fashion, there God is the reason for your coming and going to these places. That means that God is your source. He is the one to report to in times of need. He is the one to report to in times of heartache. He is the one to report to in times of pure loneliness. He is the one to talk to in times of frustration. He is the one to talk to when you feel there is no hope! But! Know these, God rules all and he is the one who also will decide how your life will and should be. You may not want to proceed with it in the manner he puts before you, but just know going against what he has put before you can cause a bad rash, in so many words. My word of encouragement to you comes from God and the Holy Spirit. I would never tell you any different than it is. However, you have to be the one to truly find out for yourself.

Lesson 5
The Truth of Ones Self-Ability

Your Value is very high. No matter what the cost is for you, you are just priceless. How priceless are you? Don't let money be your main fame and focus that you cannot proceed to have a joyful life without. We need money pretty much to live on, but, does it make life all itself? I mean should that be so concentrated on that we lose control in all that is us because of the mighty dollar bill? I see all of us as a priceless piece of jewel. If we were to describe ourselves to others I know I would say, "I want a most precious gem that is more than all the money you may hand over to anyone. That's what I feel about myself.

The Truth of Ones Self-Ability is this: Knowing How, Learning to, Enjoying when, and having With. Think about it!

Lloyd John Ogilvie says, "The greatest Counselor in the world is our Armorbearer. Who equips us with the whole armor of God for the battle with Satan".

Paulette G. Cohen known as "inspiration"

"There is a truth that gives us special strength for the battle; when we belong to Jesus Christ we are surrounded by a protective seal".

Quotes from the book The Greatest Counselor in the World.

"I'm not living lies no matter how comfortable they may be.

I really feel that I'm too old for both abstractions and games,

I will not shut off any of my essential sources of power, control and knowledge. I learned to speak the truth by accepting many Parts of myself and making them serve one another". Audre Lorde:

Part I

A Gathering of the Hearts

Since we have grown through the last few lessons, How do you feel? About you? I mean right now!! What do you think you have accomplished? Believe me when I say throughout my words of spiritual encouragement and advice, you actually taught yourself. We all have it in us to fulfill any necessary need we are deserving of. You have opened your heart, soul, mind, and body to all Gods goodness. Be proud of you!

One thing I must tell you, which is very important, is to never be afraid to compliment yourself, or give yourself credits for all you have done and made progress of. As I said before, when you do that, you are still giving praise to the almighty! Why? because there is God in you! So scream, praise his name aloud, jump for joy, and yell. Let the world know how he has graced you with all of his wonderful and wondrous ways of goodness. You believed in yourself throughout this journey. You knew that you could do this. You have become a totally different person, so guess what? You can rest assure your life has a whole new meaning to others but most important, yourself. You have begun to uplift your soul in the most rejoicing way. A feeling of newness is in store for you.

The light of good is on from now until eternity. You did that, because you allowed the sun to continue to shine about your loving and gracious self. You are so beautiful, please know that! You are what you feel. We spend so much time being insecure, that we don't take the time to see ourselves. It's ok to say thank you to yourself. Every time you do that, look into the mirror of your soul and remember you are thanking the God in you.

It's time now to go shopping. Where do we want to go? Let's search for quality just as we are; women of quality. Doesn't that sound good? We can be in touch with each other for ideas on what looks good for each one of us. Helping one another as we grow, as sisters in faith will help us to share ideas, because we have softened our hearts, but strengthened our minds! We are not threatened what others look like, and jealousy does not play a role in our lives. We are strong individuals, willing and able to strive to the top without stepping on our fellow sisters who have not gotten there yet, however, we will be working with them too.

We will not! And I say will not! Ever look down on a person who may not still believe in how we have accomplished these things. You will run into non-believers. You will run into people who cannot understand what has come across our type. We have not turned into something unusual, we just blossoms so bright that we look different to others, but trust me when I say this, it's all-good! You will become flexible. Wanting to help more people. Sky's the limit; your grasp on life as a whole will be remarkable.

Does this sound like something you never thought or dreamed would happen to you? Take a good look at yourself now since the beginning, haven't you changed? If you can't see it, then neither can I.

I want you lovely ladies to understand this, we are truly sisters. I have adopted you in my heart, without really knowing you at all. What I do know is, God is calling us. Some of you can't hear. Well let me tell you if there is a problem with your ears, I have a bull horn nice and loud and that is one of the many things I was blessed with to help share these thoughts with you.

One day God said to me, go out and tell those like yourself that I am hear to give some light to their lives. I could not figure out where to start. In my mind, I came across some new beginnings and how I got there. I prayed and ask God to help me get to the correct destination in life. God guided me to a whole new level in love, renews, spirituals and the height of meaningless attitude. Thanks be to the man above for all the blessings bestowed upon my family and me.

I also want to share something personal with you ladies. On October 11 1990 I lost my mother to a sudden stroke right in the home I reside in today. My mother was one of the strongest women in life I knew. She had character, Godliness, love, inspiration, thoughtfulness, care, and everything someone would dream about in becoming a mother. I struggled with growing up being the youngest child. We were brought up in a small church somewhere near park Ave. My sisters and I sang in the choir as children. I remember the preacher anointing our heads with oil every Sunday, however, as we grew a little older we changed the church we were going to.

We began to go to a church on 7th Ave. and 131st St. Willams Institution AME Church. Once again we were in the choir. I was young at the time, but I loved to sing. At the age of 13 my aunt ask my mother about coming to her church which was, Abyssinian Baptist Church located at 138th St. Once my family started going there, we knew that was going to be our rest stop. God said, "Here you are", we were suppose to be they're for a long time. At the age of 19, I decided to receive God in my life through the waters. I was baptized! Not to long after, other members of my family also decided to give their lives to God.

I continued to go to church for a while as long as my mother took me. After my mother died, I had a hard time accepting that God had taken her away from me. What could I have possibly done so wrong that my mother had to be taken away. We were at the height of our relationship as mother and daughter, so why would he do this? It took me almost three years to come to grip with the facts as to why this happened. But, to say all that, I will tell you sisters this. I had to learn all about standing on my own and giving faith to God as a child turned into and adult. What I was blessed with from my mother is she took me to God as a young girl, and instilled the values I have today. I have learned to appreciate what God has done to open my eyes to becoming a true spiritual and growing sister in faith.

I have come to the waters as a child and swam across the ways. In the time period I was sulking because of the lost of my mother, I learned to become a woman. Thanks be to God for this.

About five years ago, I found God all over again. One day I said 'lord I need you"! I said it in my heart. What I knew was this, since I lost my mother, God has watched over my loving father, my children, and me. God has made me grow up. I know what it feels like to receive his love in the goodness of my heart. I have never denied what he wanted to give to me. If there was a question about my needs, he was there. I never had to ask. My mother has still been around me, for a long period of time. She has guided me out of danger. I have felt her presence. I have seen her, I have smelled her. I know God has her under his wing, after all, where else would she be?

I feel the need to tell you ladies this about me because I want you to understand God loves you even if you don't love yourself. However, it feels much better to see why God loves you. You might never know the answer to that, but know this, you are a loving, blessing child born onto this earth from dust to dust. Our souls are alive and open. When all is well and we are gone, dust will be dust again, but where the soul is left is the question.

Ask yourself this, where do I want my soul to be left? My body is gone but, where will my soul live? I want mine to live with my mother to be reunited. How about you?

"Men always want to change things, and women probably don't.

I don't think it has much to do with women's powerlessness.

Change could be death. You don't have to change everything. Some

Things should be just the way they are. Under the guise of change

And love, you destroy all sorts of things, each other, children. Toni Morrison:

Romans: 8:2-5
For the law of the Spirit of life in Christ Jesus
hath made me free from the law of sin and death.
For what the law could not do, in that it was weak
through the flesh, God sending his own Son in
the likeness of sinful flesh, and for sin
condemned sin in the flesh.
That the righteousness of the law might be fulfilled in
us, who walk not after the flesh,
But after the Spirit.
For they are after the flesh do mind the things of the
flesh; but they that are
After the Spirit, the things of the Spirit.

Paulette G. Cohen known as "inspiration"

Part II

Paulette G. Cohen known as "inspiration"

The Positive Journey

Negativity! how do one bring this upon themselves. Very easy; I will not predict what is suppose to happen because I really don't know. Why bring it to yourself? We are in control of what is up and what we want up! Do not second-guess life's situations. It is not always going to be the worst. You can make it the best. You can take a corrective charge and go full force with great order. You! You! You! the positive energy only will exert if you allow it to. You are born from the positive light from above. Whatever acts you decide to follow is up to you. If you`decide to go left at a right light then it's up to you to correct that turn. Live your life positively for no upsets to proceed. Live the unlimited life with God always on your side.

When you hear those circles that surround you with spots saying the wrong things, it is so easy to wake up from the dawn into the light and lime of sunshine and say, "this was a nightmare awaiting to enter the dome".

Then pull yourself up and just refuse. Keep saying, keep talking, I want to be more like you, oh yes I do.

There is a crisis at times that requires some people to panic, lose control, worry, stress out and all of the above. What do you do? A crisis coming along, you don't know what the next step may be? What should I do? What's going to happen to my family? What if? What if? All so irrelevant to concern yourself about that it can drive you crazy. Well here is a great solution to the problem/problems, there will come a time where you may come across some misfortune but can do it. You can keep going to the bitter end. It is sometimes your time to shine, just be patient and wait.

Now that you are shining, lets turn the lights down a little. You have your chest stuck out, head up, what's up with that? Are you quote on quote trying to be better than anyone else as another person may say? All it is, is you are finally coming out of that shell you have been tucked in all your life. Someone pays you a compliment and you just don't know what to say, well, how about just thank you. We have to learn to except that we are true blue beauties in the eyes of the beholder, which is holding up this world that we are a part of. Beauty yes beauty is not only skin deep but deeper than you can imagine it would be. To love yourself in the way you should love yourself can come across the wrong way if you don't know how to love yourself correctly.

Now how should I love myself the right way you say? Here is the way? Don't abuse anything about you that are most precious. Never pass judgement on yourself and no one else. No that you deserve just as much if not better than anyone else, because you are important in Gods eyes and yours. Be careful of what you put out to anyone else as to point the finger towards him or her unless you want them to be pointed back at you.

End of a workday you feel a little on the stress side of certain aggravation that is normal, because of the way a job can get to you. We don't let it for we know it is only temporary. We have not programmed our minds to keep us under the gun. We will not let the Jones get to us; it is not in our soul. No matter what the situation may be, we have made an agreement with ourselves. We will not allow the demon seed enter our womb. Hello again my favorite world, it's so nice to be a part of you. Me, I consider myself to be a brown princess. The glow of spirit has risen in me. I step up to self-the way God has taught me to do. I have grown to love myself for who I am and the way I was put on this earth.

I have my own ideas about my life. I put my mind in the right order for me to continue to keep going on, as I should. How blessed are you? Let me count the ways. How wonderful you are? Let me show you the ways. How lovely can you be? Let me guide you through the channels.

We have grown so much larger in our own world with God holding our hands. His precious love is the best thing to come upon. I walk in the dignity that shows my grace of blackness. I know the next current event to take place will be the stars in my eyes which will enlighten more of you than anything will. I know I am blessed. I know I am a

beautiful being that has blossomed into a buxom princess. God whispers to me all the time to hold his names to the highest and never give up!

"The map for your life is within you. Go there to find the way". This powerful visualization will help you welcome change and move forward in faith; see yourself joyful, laughing, running toward yourself, your arms flung wide, the wind at your back. Know that wherever you are you always in Gods embrace, soaring toward your destiny, on your way home. Susan Taylor; Publication Director, Essence Magazine.

Part III

Paulette G. Cohen known as "inspiration"

Acknowledging the Belief-Growing as a Strong African American Heritage Woman

Amazing it is being as who we should be and glowing in the most magnificent way, and that's Gods way. Now that the universe as a whole has entered into our lives what do we expect to happen? We will make what the best will be. Full Figured African American Women on the spiritual journey and the road to success can be very inspiring to other people of this heritage and for that matter all cultures.

Let's talk about the meaning to up holding ourselves in the light of honor to one another. What do we mean by up holding ourselves to the light of honor to other individuals? The respect of knowing that we all share a common bond of loving God and the God within all of us. The work will be done automatically to gain the success we have inside, also to achieve the best in life. When glowing all over to shine around the inevitable is one of the most marvelous things we may due as a universal tribute to life itself.

Well, we are almost done and we owe it all to ourselves. We have excepted that life is full of choices that we have to make for no one but ourselves, if we thump across an error or so, then let's not blame anyone else, correct? Get up kiss yourself for arriving at the decision that you have made a wrong turn and ask the infinite what is the next move. After you have received his answer, you take it from there.

Remember to continue to exercise your mind to gain the fullest that life has for you. Make yourself conscious that we all need someone, and that person is God. Get into a program where others will encourage you because we share a common bond all together.

You beautiful creatures, life is enriching because of our beauty. Lots of love, lots of fun, lots of spirit, lots of sharing, we all have as one. Prayer works! Never let anyone tell you different. Praying is the ultimate in surviving anything. Talking to the almighty is lovely, because of the comfortable light he shine around during the process of elimination. The warm comforts that you exercise while releasing your soul in his hands. The wave of a new day has risen because you hear his voice. Meditate on him and see the amazing outcome that has been laid to rest in your honor.

Everything I am telling you is to get you use to being in control of your own minds. Don't get fooled by what others who have not found themselves are trying to say. Don't be discouraged about what you truly want. Don't be afraid to ask for it. Ask and you shall receive! Knock and the door will open! Seek and yea shall find! God will answer all.

Spirit being alive and well is what will make all of us notice what we truly need out of life. Where we will present ourselves to the public and to our family and friends the right way as a large woman. I say the right way because, as I said before that we can get very lax and comfortable that we don't continue our process of growing the right way and *keeping our appearance the way to get the respect that we deserve.*

What our true accomplishments are getting what Gods feels we deserve? Being one of his great creations deserve only the best. Back in one of my chapters I mentioned a person who will except anything from their partners such as infidelity just to make up excuses to stay with that one. Well, most of the time when we set our frame of mind to think in that manner we tend to make it happen.

A lot of times in life we full figured women get so focused on the fact that if we can even get someone we should except them for who they are, being that they have excepted us as we are. Therefore, when that person does not have a job and thinks he or she may depend on you to live their life because they are the king or queen and you should be grateful that they are even with you, should not be excepted in the first place. Who do they think they are? They should be happy that we are with them, and furthermore need to get a job! When those same type of people decide that they should explore other opportunities with other women or men because of the same mentality as the above, you can say go take a hike. We have to learn to think of ourselves first not the other person. No type of guilt trip should make any of us feel we should take anything less than the best from other people. It really bothers me when I see this insecure type of behavior. It's pure low self-esteem.

I'm not trying to beat up on you ladies, but I must tell you this to let it stick within. There are to many times when we think that our weight is beyond control for other people to except. When a person chooses someone to be a part of their life, they except them for who they are, whether they are thin, large, tall, short, or whatever. A lot of times we can become so comfortable with our partners tat we can meet someone a certain way and let go of ourselves thinking, well, I already got him or her so I don't have to look the same as I did when I met them. This is not true! One thing we must learn, that is even though we do not need to dress to impress the person you are involved with, we should dress to *impress ourselves! On the other hand we also must keep our partner interested in who we are to remind them why they fell in love with us, whether it's inside or outside.*

All this is pure spiritual growth. Once we feel good about ourselves because we took God up on his offer to come to him for everything we need know, our life automatically over turned. God said come to me and let your life begin in a divine order, and that's all the more reason why you should. His unconditional love for you makes life more meaningful then you will ever know.

One of the strongest quotes I have came to hear was from Sonia Sanchez, a well-known writer/poet. She states this:

"Sisters tell me today that when they go out for jobs they straighten their hair, because if they go in with their hair natural or braided, they probably won't get the job. So I say, "How can you let someone dictate to you how you're going to look. The reason we went through what we did is so that one group or people would no longer dictate to another group, because if a country can tell a people, the way it used to tell black people a few years ago, you must look a certain way. Then it is complete control over you!

Paulette G. Cohen known as "inspiration"

The Finale

Many days I talked to so many people who are still looking for something, but they don't really know what it is. That's because there is a missing link to their life. Sometimes we need to look beyond the normal everyday life and search for the infinite. <u>The Infinite </u>and who is he? <u>The Almighty</u> and who is he? <u>The Greatest Love in the World</u>, and who is he? <u>The Man Above</u> and who is he you asked? All these questions come to your mind when you just don't know. It is time for you to find out don't you think? It is time to open up your hearts, soul, mind, and body to the temple of life and realize it cannot get any better until you allow him to come directly into your world, and receive his holy name.

I love to shed true light to people in need to release that negative energy from within. I would like to allow them to not dump on me their problems, but to let out that excessive baggage that is hanging over their heads they can't let go. I like to let them know that it's ok and that everything is going to be all right.

We all need a shoulder to cry on once in a while, some more than others do.

A gift, how important is that to you? Being a gift to yourself, how important is that to you? Being a gift to the infinite, how important is that to you? All of the above should be, very important, because you are a gift and a mighty one!

Life is good! Life is sweet! Life is what you make it! How would you set your life to be? Think real careful about this, because when I spoke to you in the other chapters, I explained how important the thinking process is. Now let me re-phrase what I just said. How important is your life to you? Mines is very important because I have the Spirit of holiness guiding me in the right direction.

Ladies and gentlemen, Wake Up! And smell the coffee and if helps drink it! If someone wants to walk you through times that can only help you, then I say go for it. The problem we have today is, not many people want to help others. Sometimes a simple hold of the hand to help someone across the streets is all it takes. You will be surprise what people will not do today to extend him or herself to help someone else, because it just is too much for him or her.

I truly wish this world could be a better place to live at, where people would not depend on happiness from others. They would know not only how to keep themselves happy, but to make people who are in need happy also. That is what is missing today, finding true happiness within you.

A lot of women seek happiness from men: they feel if they get involved with a man it will make their life complete. Why should it take anyone to make your life complete?

God is the only one in this world that makes your life complete and you! If your life is going to be incomplete, then no one but you can make it! Think about that!

What happens is, women who think like the above always find the wrong person to get into a relationship with and it never works. They think they are able to change the person, to who they may fantasize about or have a baby to keep them around, or even worse literally hold them at close range, so

they may not even look at anyone else. This is what you call pure low self-esteem!

Let's not let that happen to you. Make your life worth while without anyone but you who is most important!

The Epilogue

In conclusion to this guide, I just want to say thank you for allowing me to be a part of your lives. God sent the message out, and the Spirit carried it through me. I f there were any type of living that I was willing to receive it would be to do this all over again. I really think though that many of us are learning better today than yesterday. Be it as it may: we must truly find that special one above to inspire us to move on to a better grace in our lives in order to maintain and better ourselves.

There is a lesson to be learned and a story always to be told in someone's life. Just remember this: never judge anyone else's and please do not compare the two. We are extraordinary individuals. We were placed here to learn from one to another.

Thanks be to God for this golden opportunity. Thanks be to God for all of ladies, women, and children. Thanks be to God for the conciensous choice he gives us to make. Thanks be to God for all humanity.

Thanks be to God for being our savior. Thanks be to God for heading my life. Thanks be to God for allowing me to be of some justice to you. Thanks be to God for trusting me enough to put care in my hands to distribute among many. Thanks be to God for having faith in me. Thanks be to God we have been brought together now as a family. Thanks be to God for giving me health and strength to carry on these messages. Thanks be to God for walking with me through some of my hard times during this period. Thanks be to God for showing me some individuals who needs to hear this message loud and clear. Thanks be to God for opening up my eyes also to the needs written in this book. Thanks be to God for helping me gain some knowledge from this experience. Thanks be to God for my daily guidance. Thanks be to God for all the wonderful people he put in my life who have done nothing but support this project from day one. Thanks be to God for the message that was sent out to me as well. Thanks be to God for his son Jesus that sacrificed so much to make me whole today.

Thanks be to God to the people, places and things I had to encounter throughout this journey to get me where I am today. Thanks be to God for all of him.

The next thing on the agenda is this: I will be conducting a support group, which will be in focus to what I have spoken on in this book. It is important that we continue to believe in ourselves as I mentioned. Therefore we will continue the growing faith and open up to each other.

It's not over because the book has an ending; this is just the beginning. We have a long way to go. Remember that our minds have opened now, so let's get on the good foot. We are in the presence of each other so let's loosen up and be frank with one another. That is what we are here for.

The next move will be up to God in reference to what I'm to do.

"when you work to obtain greater awareness, knowledge and understanding of yourself, you are working for God"! Quote from Iyanla Vanzants novel Acts of Faith

Paulette G. Cohen known as "inspiration"

My Personal dedications to our young sisters out there.

Hello beautiful big ladies or even women who feel like what I mentioned in this guide: I have provided a gift just for you.

The following pages are several poems written so you may take a good look at yourself and think about how valuable you are.

Some may be what you need to hear; the others are just you!

Big and Beautiful

Tall, short, or whatever
You stand out even in bad weather
That is you all the way
It doesn't matter what anyone has to say
You are so gifted and talented by far
When the going gets tough, that's where
You are.
Big and Beautiful and lovely all over
Is like finding a 4 leaf clover.
Stay dynamic, lovely and all
When you walk out, you'll have a ball!
So don't be sad about any little thing,
Because it will be your tune
Everyone else has to sing.

Strong

We are strong in every aspect of life.
Our courage, motivation and spunkiness
can make us a good wife.
The strength we demonstrate is very right.
Sometimes we can't help, but shine
   without light.
Look at you for who you are.
There is no other, you are a star!
Deep inside your glowing full range.
It's just a matter of hidden change.
Now don't you ever give up on you,
With strength like yours, you'll know
what to do.

Mistakes

We are not a mistake!
A mistake is something not meant to happen.
We are here because we are supposed to be.
Mistakes are made because of carelessness.
We were born to love and be loved with a lot of love.
Now wait one minute if you ever knew anything,
This big girl here has plenty to say!
The unique features that's in our heart, is what makes us so gorgeous, so a mistake Heck NO!
Never, we definitely were supposed to be!

Just a Little Free

Being free for who you are and should be
Is what we can do today.
Not like a long time ago when there was
 limited
Places to stay.
I love being free for who I am, don't you?
There is so much my life is worth and what
I can do.
Free to love, free to have a choice, and
 free
To whirl around.
I am so fee, I could run and jump up and
Down.
The spirit has lifted my soul so high.
I can't stand to say good-bye
I know one day my time will come.
At least I know I was free more than some.

Sexy

The thighs she has are so nice and shapely
When she walks in front of the guys,
They can't help but open their eyes wide.
This big girl stands about 5'11 dark and
  all!
She has a big butt curvy and tall.
She knows her stuff is very special,
Because God built her the way to show
  others
She is all a queen should be.
So when you see this type of girl,
Bow down to her she is a real pearl!

Within

Deep within our spirit is a well known
Person that
We
Never would suspect could
Occur.
It is so well hidden
That
Even the
Slightest feeling
Does not damage
It.
At times, we need to
Just reach
For that small piece
That is missing.
Can you find yours?
Once you have
Located it, don't
Give up on
What it can
Do for
You!

Needing

Everyone needs someone to love.
Neither small or large
it comes from above.
Never be afraid to ask for what you want.
It is your life that no
one will haunt.
Needing more is what is true.
Feeling ugly can make
you blue.
Things are so real the more you see,
We need each other
And a place to be.
It's ok to need a friend,
They will be there
Until the end.
So when times are harder than before
Look into your soul
And believe there is no more.
God is wonderful and always great!
He is your savior and
Your soul mate!

Believing in He

She who believes in he will go far.
She who believes in herself leaves no scar.
It them who believes the best will be.
Let the positive over ride all negative to
  see.
Believe in the system you can't go wrong
Believe in yourself, realize you are strong!
Believe in your family that will stand by.
Believe they are there even if they are gone
And in the sky.
The power of he is worth the wait.
The more you believe the less you hate.
Don't give up on your belief.
This is the only sign of relief.

God Bless you all!
"inspiration"

Ladies when I wrote this book I did not know some of the tragedy that was about to occur in the future. When I finally decided to have it published this particular event just happened, The most horrific thing I have ever experienced was the terrorist act of the World Trade Center and all the people who were killed and injured during it.

I want to take this time to give my personal condolences to all the people out there who lost a friend or family member that happened to be a part of this most horrific experience. Life is a wonderful thing and when you lose so much and so many people it takes a lot out of you.

I happened to be fortunate and so blessed to be able to share this piece with all of you that are blessed to be able to be here this day to read it.

Love comes in many different directions and in many ways. We must hold our heads up high in order to bite down on that animosity we have in our heart. It should not take this type of tragedy to open our eyes to forgive others. Have your heart open right now to extend a hand or two to your neighbor or a long lost loved one. It is time for unity. It may be the only chance you will have to do it.

I ask all of you to please take a little of your time and ask God and the Spirit within to take the good that is stored away in your precious bodies and put it to good use. Help yourself and others that you can. Be and inspiration to someone. Because we know there is a lot of love out here. They're is so much of you that I don't think you even know about yourself.

It should not take something as tragic as what happened to the many people involved during the moment of this event for us to realize that God is always there. Those of us who reach out to him during moments such as this one is good, but what about other times? I have lived for many years and been around many people, places and things and it never seize to amaze me how negative people are. I am a true believer and I know God is about love. He loves you! That's why you should realize that you can turn to him at all times not just during a moment of crisis or times when someone is dying that you know.

I take a lot of this very personal because I am around people that throughout the time they are here they really do not believe in people or themselves. The sarcasm is so over whelming. But there are many people that know where it is coming from. God and his wonderful son Jesus and the power of the Holy Spirit is where it is at!

I have repeated myself over and over again but I must stress to you at this time how important it is to find it in your hearts to love. Always know there is a higher ground to walk on. There is no mountain to high to climb. And without God in your life you are nothing!

So, please be true to each other but most of all, you!

Peace, love, and all the blessings you can receive. *"inspiration"*

Paulette G. Cohen known as "inspiration"

ABOUT THE AUTHOR

Writer, Motivational Speaker, Poet.

Inspiration was born in Harlem, USA 1962. She took Business Administration at La Guardia Community College in Queens .New York, but that's not where she learned to achieve who she is today. "My true teachings came from God!" She still resides in New York with her two children. Her motive is to help reach out and rebuild Harlem in a way that will educate all individuals in particularly African American Women. "I find that a lot of my sisters out there have a lot to learn about themselves and how much they can achieve in there own self-growing. I want to lend them a hand out of my heart to show them what they did not even know they were capable of doing".

Inspiration has served on several committees affiliated with District Five School Board and is an active member of the Abyssinian Baptist Church in Harlem, and studied spiritual growth at Unity in Lincoln

Center. Her first novel entitled **A Guide on Spiritual Growth, How Should the African American Full Figured Woman Respect Her Inner Self as well As Her Personal Appearance** *teaches individuals about loving themselves from within first, so that the outside can reflect on what's inside. She teaches workshops for individuals about self-improvement and how to love themselves not by one thing only but all over.*

Her second novel **The Love in Life Listening With Over 100 Soulful Poetry of Inspiration** *(which currently is in stores), is some of the best poems you will read based on parts of her life as well as anyone's. "Poetry is a gift that I feel all of us can appreciate no matter what the writer is saying. The sultry side of poetry can stimulate anyone's mind when looked deep into what the poet is saying. I find some of the poems I have written are apart of anyone's life experience one way or another, but the best of it is about sharing to the world".*

She is currently working on her third novel titled **This is Dedicated to the One I**

Love! Very sexy and sultry love poems for the lover in you. Inspiration *is a very versatile woman in much of what she does. She believes strongly within herself and all what she is capable of. The sensuous side of her nature combined with her spirituality makes her work more appealing to the eye!* "*I believe in the power of love and all it's worth. That's what life is about!*"